Always First Class

ALWAYS FIRST CLASS
The Pleasure of Personal Letters

Lois Barry

Always First Class: The Pleasure of Personal Letters
Copyright 2009 by Lois Barry

Acknowledgments:

Boston Museum of Fine Arts for permission to reproduce Mary Cassatt's drypoint and color aquatint, "The Letter" 1890-91.
Chicago Tribune, selection from Bob Greene.
Christian Science Monitor, selections from Leslie Katz and Sasha Quinton.
Middlebury Magazine, selection from Mel Yoken.
New York Times, selections from Letters to the Editor by Robin Ingram, Lisa Chipolone Romeo and Nancy Wait.
New York Times, selections from Vivian Gornick and Patricia Mainardi.
O, The Oprah Magazine, selection from Kate Spade.
The Oregonian, selections from Jim Carmin, Shawn Donley and about Mary Alice Bishop.
Random House, for permission to quote from Elizabeth Berg's novel, *The Pull of the Moon*.
Joan I. Siegel for permission to reprint her poem, "Mary Cassatt, 1890-1891."
Stanford Magazine, selection from Carolyn Laub.
Wall Street Journal, selection from Timothy Aeppel.
Washington Post, selection from Linton Weeks.
Writer's Digest, selection from InkWell.

Essays, collection and arrangement ©2009 Lois Barry

ISBN 978-0-9823904-0-5

Library of Congress Control Number: 2009905087

Barry, Lois
Always First Class: The Pleasure of Personal Letters
p. cm.

1. Letter-Writing 2. Quotations
I. Barry, Lois II. Title

Cover and book design: Kristin Summers, redbat design, La Grande, Oregon
Chapter Titles set in 24pt. Harrington. Text set in 12pt. Chaparral Pro.
Published by Best Letters Press
        La Grande, OR 97850
Printed in United States of America

1 2 3 4 5 6 7 8 9 10

Contents

The letter, written in absorbed solitude, is an act of faith...
To write a letter is to be alone with my thoughts in the conjured presence
of another person. I keep myself imaginative company.
I occupy the empty room. I alone infuse the silence.

—Vivian Gornick

Every one of us has experiences to share and wisdom to impart.
Let us all then leave behind letters of love and friendship,
family and devotion, hope and consolation, so that future
generations will know what we valued and achieved.

—Marian Wright Edelman

One of life's happy moments is indeed hearing someone say
"There's some important mail for you today."
Yes, letters are intended for keeps.
They are for saving, rereading and rethinking.
Many make the heart leap with laughter, jubilation, and delight.
So "reach out," find a pen, and write to someone today.

—Mel Yoken

Some say "No one writes letters anymore"

If your list of five favorite things doesn't include receiving a letter from an old friend, it's probably been so long you've forgotten how much you love it. For me, finding a personal letter mixed in with the day's business envelopes and throwaways makes the world seem brighter—it's flattering to be remembered, and I'm eager to read all about friends' families and projects and ideas. Of course I enjoy everyday e-mail and phone calls, but finding a real letter in the mailbox is even better. E-mail is a cheerful greeting waved from across the room; a letter is a friend coming over to sit down for a pleasant conversation. Better than a phone call, a letter can be set aside until I have some quiet moments to appreciate it. Then, after I've read a letter once, I save it to read and think about again before I send an answer. Usually, I put letters away to save forever.

These days, personal letters are moving toward the endangered species list. Compared to melting glaciers and faltering economies, this matter of missing correspondence is a minor issue, but it's a loss, nevertheless. We need to cherish the happy moments in our lives. Fortunately, this is one problem with an easy solution. In less than an hour we can write a letter that will make a special friend feel really good, in fact good enough to write us back!

"I used to write letters," you say. "Now I don't have time." Isn't that ironic? We're so busy with our personal computers, cell phones and BlackBerries, all of them designed to make our hectic lives easier. E-mail, text messages and cell-phone chats have become the fast foods of our daily communications, and most of us rely on these quick exchanges. But there are so many of them! Depending on our ages and inclinations, we tweet, we Facebook, we blog, we e-mail, we talk—from seldom to almost all the time. This instant socializing is crowding out the individual style and thoughtful substance of personal correspondence. We've reached a cultural tipping point where electronic and wireless contacts are about to replace even the idea of sitting down to write a letter. That's a shame. It's not only a tragedy for dedicated letter lovers, but a loss for young people who may not ever know what they're missing.

That's why hearing that 'no one writes letters any more' is a splendid reason to dust off our address books and start shopping for interesting stamps and stationery. We enjoy variety in our lives—new people, foreign foods and the latest ways of staying in touch—but we've always valued the comfort of familiar favorites, too. In the spirit of appreciating family gatherings and school reunions, summer camping trips and mom's home-cooking, I recommend a return to the nostalgic pleasures of writing and receiving real letters in real envelopes. Call it snail mail, if you must, or better: vintage, or retro or old-fashioned, or best: time-honored. The point is that like most things we've enjoyed for a very long time, private personal correspondence is definitely worth continuing.

Writing a letter gives us a chance to slow down. In the midst of a day's demanding activities, it's relaxing to retreat for a few minutes to the privileged space the universe reserves for letter writers. When James Thurber and his wife lived in Paris during World War II, he wrote that when the bombs started to fall, "Helen will lean out the window and say *Cut that out! My husband is trying to write a letter!*" Let the world take note: letter writers deserve respect. No matter how we write, soft pencil on notebook paper, fine pen on smooth stationery or clicking along at the keyboard, we're in charge. It's restful to start a quiet conversation on paper, reading our words as they appear on the page, smiling as we report events, share thoughts or send congratulations.

This is an ideal time to revisit the easy art of writing letters. You'll be participating in a valued tradition, what one of the world's great letter writers referred to as "delicious conversations." You can put on your informal writing clothes and be chatty and spontaneous or dress up a little and be reflective and deliberate. As you tailor your messages to delight the tastes of your individual correspondents, there's an excellent opportunity to be creative. You'll never find a more appreciative audience for your writing talents. Beautiful cards with handwritten messages, sketchy greetings written on lined paper with doodles in the margins, elegant notes on stylish stationery or hefty manila envelopes stuffed with typed pages, clippings and photographs—all approaches are welcome. When the letter is finished, it's immensely satisfying to drop it in the mail slot. Signed, sealed, and soon to be delivered—a unique gift of your time.

Once your letter is in the mail, you can look forward to friends' happy surprise at receiving it. "I know that handwriting! Look at that lovely stamp!" "Well, open it up! See what she says!" There it will be—a genuine personal letter with folded pages in a sealed envelope—no jingling, no texting, no mass mailing, an absolutely private message hand-delivered, anywhere in the world. (That's impressive service for the price of a postage stamp.) If the planets are properly aligned, once your friends have read and discussed the pages you've written just for them, they will be inspired to write you back! And so begins a delicious conversation. Simply put, writing letters and receiving them is still a very nice thing to do.

I'd rather mingle souls by letter
than live a life of regret through email.

—Simon Jenkins

We've been writing letters
for a long time

A young tourist, enchanted by the architecture bordering the piazza where she sits at an outdoor café, describes the sights in a letter to friends at home. She decorates her pages with sketches and chooses colorful postage stamps to complement her letter. A business man in an airport lounge quickly pens an affectionate note to his wife. He knows she will be delighted to see his handwriting on the envelope. A grandmother writes a letter filled with memories of her early school years to a grandchild who is about to enter first grade. She smiles, picturing her grandson's parents reading her letter aloud and discussing it with him.

Whenever we write a personal letter, we continue a delightful tradition of correspondence that initially flourished more than three hundred years ago during the reign of Louis XIV. At that time, having the leisure and the education to write a personal letter was valued as a sign of prosperity and of rare personal freedom. Although the opulent life-style of the French court—lavish banquets and masked balls for six-hundred weekend guests— is long past, the private activity of writing letters has remained relatively unchanged. It's remarkable to consider that centuries of experimentation and social progress were necessary before we could enjoy something as pleasantly uncomplicated as the exchange of personal letters.

As long as five thousand years ago, various permanent but cumbersome writing surfaces were being developed: silk scrolls in China, then clay tablets in Mesopotamia, papyrus along the Nile, and wax tablets and vellum in Greece and Imperial Rome. We've come a long way from using a stick to make marks in wet clay, and thoughts of using vellum as a writing surface ("First, procure the skin of a sheep or goat...") should make us eternally grateful for paper.

At first, people used writing to record simple tallies of crops and taxes and battlefield successes. Then as languages and societies became more complex, details of monumental construction projects, histories and political mandates, inspirational literature and philosophical doctrines were written down. Writing was a laborious process, reserved for safeguarding the most important information.

As Western civilization developed, those in positions of power realized that people who could read and write tended to be more difficult to control, so access to literacy was rigorously limited to select individuals within the province of the Catholic Church. Political and religious leaders—often illiterate themselves—dictated essential messages to secretaries whose very lives depended on their fidelity and discretion. Monasteries and the royal houses of Europe maintained their own delivery systems for official correspondence, and interfering with mail couriers was punishable by death. In those times the exchange of letters was reserved for the powerful.

In the 15th century, as the absolute control of the church began to decline, the first relatively inexpensive smooth paper was being manufactured in England. Rough, cheap paper had been made in small quantities for centuries but was not widely used because long-lasting vellum was preferred. After 1440, the availability of durable paper combined with the invention of movable-type presses made printed books affordable for the first time. Additional small numbers of people learned to read and write, and the private exchange of personal letters without an intermediary finally became a possibility.

Even so, because the majority of people still remained illiterate, separated family members depended on street-corner scribes to write down their messages to distant loved ones. Their small folded missives, scrawled on scraps of paper, were entrusted to travelers who carried each letter as close to the destination as possible, then handed it off to someone else—usually another pilgrim, crusader, wandering monk or itinerant performer—who then passed the letter along to still other travelers until it finally reached its destination. It's no wonder people at that time believed in miracles. What else could explain actually receiving a tattered letter that had been passed through so many hands over such long distances for so many months!

During the 17th century everything changed. In the newly prosperous Netherlands and in the court of Louis XIV, literacy flourished as the intellectual freedom of the Reformation merged with the aesthetic delights of the Renaissance. Merit and ability achieved parity with rank and privilege. At Versailles and in the salons of Paris, educated women enthusiastically asserted their independence by embracing letter writing as an amusing means of self expression. Aristocratic ladies, dressed in silk and satin gowns, whiled away their afternoons writing at small desks inlaid with ivory and precious woods, exchanging tidbits of court gossip and the details of their days with friends and family in neighboring chateaux.

The French court's passion for letter writing was so pervasive that the king issued an edict standardizing the size of paper so it could be folded conveniently into the square envelopes of the day. At that time, letter writing evolved from being a necessity for official long distance communication to serving as a favored form of recreation, an elegant occupation for agile minds seeking a diversion from the routine of daily activities.

The new vogue of personal letter writing soon spread from France and the Netherlands across Europe and to England where once again it was adopted as a refined social pursuit by the privileged classes, charmed by their participation in "lettered sociability." In English society the quantity and quality of correspondence became an indicator of one's social standing. Mail was so important that the city of London provided three mail deliveries each day.

For the next two hundred years, writers perfected their correspondence styles, inventors addressed the challenging task of creating envelopes that would seal properly, and diligent bureaucrats standardized postal rates and improved mail delivery procedures, eventually creating the postal system we enjoy today.

During that time, American colonists and later immigrants to the United States were sending letters to those left behind in the old country and to those who had fanned out in every direction to explore and settle the new land. Politicians, abolitionists, soldiers, suffragettes, lonely women exchanging family news, working men far from home, all documented the conditions of their daily lives to distant friends and families in their letters. It's not surprising that the Pony Express briefly became the icon of communication as settlers moved west.

Throughout the last century, members of the Armed Forces, mobile young

American families, college students, Peace Corps volunteers, vacationers, adventure travelers and overseas workers among many others depended upon the mails to stay in touch.

Compared to all the generations of letter writers that have preceded us, we enjoy a remarkable wealth of writing materials—fine papers and envelopes, pencils and pens of all kinds, typewriters and word processors—plus reliable and inexpensive mail delivery anywhere in the world. Of course we take basic literacy and freedom of expression for granted. But with all of that, only a tiny fraction of the mail now delivered to American households—about one piece per week, or less—is personal letters. Buried under a postal avalanche of catalogs, advertising circulars and monthly bills, we seem to have reached a nadir of social correspondence. Where are the letters from best friends in school, buddies in basic training, interesting neighbors who moved to another state, the remarkable couple from last year's elder hostel? How long has it been since we wrote a letter to a favorite relative or a distant friend? It's curious, the way once-precious personal correspondence has gradually dwindled without our appearing to notice its loss.

Even so, the rich tradition of writing and receiving letters endures. Dedicated writers still settle down at kitchen tables and office desks to compose messages to their letter writing partners. Eager readers stand in post office lobbies scanning handwritten pages, and women in coffee shops pull colored envelopes from their purses, rereading long typed letters from distant friends.

As long as we've been writing letters—and that's a very long time—people have been writing *about* letters. The quotations in this collection have been drawn from historical documents and published letters, as well as from contemporary letters and media. The voices span several centuries and are as varied as the writers and societies that produced them. My hope is that this celebratory chorus will strike a chord, prompting you to revisit the pleasures of exchanging letters with friends and family. As a letter writer, you'll be warmly welcomed into a society of enthusiastic correspondents.

In 600 B.C., Cyrus the Great is said to have shaved slaves' heads, written important messages on them, waited for the hair to grow back, then sent the slaves off to have their heads shaved again so the messages could be read by other rulers who, one hopes, were not in a big hurry to hear from him.

...

Instructions for making vellum

First kill a goat, sheep or calf, clean and scald the skin, soak it in lime, then stretch and dry it on a frame. Scrape all the hair from the skin's surface and then smooth the skin with chalk so that it will accept ink.

...

Instructions for making ink

Gather nut galls, mix with green vitriol (sulfate of iron) and isinglass from fish bladders.

~ or ~

Mix soot from burning the wood of appropriate trees with liquid in which nuts and bark have been boiled. Strain out impurities.

Your letter arrived!

That was a fine letter and made us all feel happy here
which is what letters are supposed to do

—JOHN CHEEVER

Your letters are such fun. Your "Personal from her sister" causes a rumpus!
Commander Dam appeared one morning very proudly bearing your letter—
"from her sister"—as though he had laid an egg, and then in true
Danish gallantry he said "Is your sister as sweet as you?"
("Tum tee tum tum tum tum!") I replied, "Much sweeter."
"Well then," he said, bowing a little "I hope you will give her my regards."

—ANNE MORROW LINDBERG TO HER SISTER

A letter is the consolation of life.

—FRANCOIS VOLTAIRE

What a letter, *ma tres bonne!* What thanks I owe you
for having used your eyes, your head, your hand, your time to compose
such an agreeable [letter] for me! I read and reread it, and will reread it again
with much pleasure and attention; there is no reading in which
I can take more interest. You satisfy my curiosity about all that I wished
to hear, and I admire your care in writing me such punctual responses;
that makes for a well-regulated and delicious conversation.

—Mme de Sévigné to her daughter

Your letter arrived precisely one hour ago, and here I am sitting down
to answer it. Whether the answer will be sent is, of course,
another matter. Your last–slightly tipsy, very brilliant—sympathetic,
inspiring and the best you ever wrote,—sent me flying to the inkpot,
but when I read my production and compared it with yours
my vanity as an author refused to be pacified. I can't
endure that you should write so well...

—Virginia Woolf to Roger Fry

I was pleased to get your long letter covering wire platforms, debeaking,
coccidiosis, Belgian endive, root cellars, perpetual motion, connubial
bliss, anemia, B-12, chicken lettuce, whooping cranes and Scott Nearing.
Almost, if not quite, in that order. You asked, very kindly, how things
are going with me. They are going all right, because I am now 73, and
a man who is 73 and still up and around is doing all right...

—E. B. White to Mason Trowbridge

[Your letters] serve like gleams of light, to cheer a dreary scene where envy, hatred, malice, revenge, and all the worse passions of men are marshalled to make one another as miserable as possible.

—THOMAS JEFFERSON TO HIS DAUGHTER MARTHA

My dearest Fanny,
   You are inimitable, irresistible. You are the delight of my life. Such letters, such entertaining letters, as you have lately sent!— such a description of your queer little heart!—such a lovely display of what imagination does. You are worth your weight in gold, or even in the new silver coinage. I cannot express to you what I have felt in reading your history of yourself, how full of pity and concern and admiration and amusement I have been. You are the paragon of all that is silly and sensible, common- place and eccentric, sad and lively, provoking and interesting...

—JANE AUSTEN TO FANNY KNIGHT

Your letters are always a highlight of my day whether they are long or short. Actually, I love them all, but the longer the better is true for me. The walk home from the post office is always shorter when I stroll along reading one of your interesting, newsy, chuckle-producing letters. . . .

—MARY MCCOMBS TO LOIS BARRY

There is something special about a personal letter.
It's better than a phone call, no matter what the telephone company
says. A phone call disappears into the air as soon as the receiver
is put back on the hook. A good letter can last a lifetime.

—ANDY ROONEY

He wasn't much good on the phone. 'I sent you a letter,' he'd say, and
then there'd be a long and painful pause. What he had to say–exactly
what he had to say–was in the mail. And often his letters communicated
that which he had not, or would not have otherwise, made clear.

—BENJAMIN CHEEVER WRITING ABOUT HIS FATHER, JOHN

How beautiful your letter was! It was very full of you and it is
wonderful that you write as you are. Very few can do that, and many
who only write never learn it as long as they live. And with you writing
isn't even the main thing. [Clara Westhoff was a sculptor]...I thank you
so much and think of you in connection with only nice things.

—RAINIER MARIA RILKE TO CLARA WESTHOFF

A friendship can weather most things and thrive in thin soil;
but it needs a little mulch of letters and phone calls and small, silly
presents every so often—just to save it from drying out completely.

—PAM BROWN

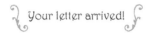

It's uplifting to get a letter—like an 'ooh!' in your mailbox.

—KATE SPADE

Barbara,
Did I ever tell you that when I receive your letters, I never open them until I've performed a little ritual. First, I make a pot of tea, then I banish everyone from the room, and finally I settle myself into the left-hand side of the living room loveseat. I savor every word, sometimes cry, often laugh, and always read the letter one more time.

Dear Lynne,
I was moved to tears by your last letter. It made me realize that my letters are as treasured by you as yours are by me. I too have a ritual when yours arrive…I would go through all the other mail, saving your letter for last and then, tea mug at the ready (yes, really) would read it s-l-o-w-l-y, sometimes titillating myself by stopping to mull things over before going on to the next paragraph. I am so pleased we have found each other, and over and above our shared pain, for we certainly are worthy of each other's friendship.

—BARBARA SHULGOLD AND LYNNE SIPIORA

[Connected through a newsletter for infertile couples, Barbara and Lynne developed a loving, supportive friendship during three years of correspondence. Both were finally successful in adopting children. They never met.]

Please write again soon. Though my own life is filled with activity, letters encourage momentary escape into others' lives and I come back to my own with greater contentment.

—Elizabeth Forsythe Hailey, in *A Woman of Independent Means*

In these days of the 'cashless society,' telephones, cables, telegrams, copier service coast-to-coast via wires or glass fibers, the private letter still has its place—and always will. Nothing—not even a phone call— can beat the permanence and personal attention implicit in every letter. Letters take time—time spent means someone cared.

—Arthur Ashe

The telephone is to the letter what television is to reading. But some of us are addicted to writing and receiving mail, and I don't see it, in the scheme of current addictions, as a particularly harmful one.

—Mary McGrory

As long as there are postmen life will have zest.

—Henry James

A priceless gift of thoughtfulness, straight from the heart in making new friends...is the luxury of a written letter.

—Alda

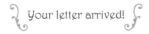

[As we traveled ten years ago] it was so exciting picking up a packet of letters from family and friends every couple of months. We'd always have a contest to see who would get the most letters. Each letter would be savored and reread several times. You can't beat e-mail for convenience, but I love the tactile feel of a letter.

—SHAWN DONLEY

I've received long text messages that I would count as letters... I also think a well crafted email counts as a letter. Of course, nothing is as intimate as a hand written letter, delivered by mail or, even better, by hand. For me, a letter is all about the amount of time and thought that the letter-writer invests. ...And I think as long as anyone exists who feels the desire to communicate in a profound way with another human being, the art of letter writing will never vanish.

—JOSH KNELMAN

 "Messenger of Sympathy and Love, Servant of Parted Friends" *is carved in stone over the entry to the main post office in Washington D.C.*

Mary Stevenson Cassatt,
American, 1844–1926

The Letter, 1890–91

Drypoint and
color aquatint

Platemark: 34.6 x 22.5 cm
(13 ⁵/₈ x 8 ⁷/₈ in.)

Sheet: 47.8 x 30.7 cm
(18 ¹³/₁₆ x 12 ¹/₁₆ in.)

Museum of Fine Arts,
Boston

Gift of William Emerson
and The Hayden
Collection—Charles
Henry Hayden
Fund, 41.803

Photograph © 2009
Museum of Fine Arts,
Boston

Mary Cassatt:
The Letter (1890-1891)
—Joan I. Siegel

All day it is with her like a song
even as she slices a breakfast orange,
brushes her hair,
shuts a window.
She is listening to it
when company calls
and she talks about yesterday's news,
pours tea,
says good-bye at the door.
Then, alone with it finally
in late afternoon,
she puts it on the desk,
arranges it
as though she were putting flowers in a vase.
Then she slips it into the envelope,
seals it with her tongue.

The sending of a letter constitutes
a magic grasp upon the future.

—Iris Murdoch

Now I'm writing to you...

Everything is good, even having to write letters,
because there are things one can write that one can't say just
as there are things one can say that one can't write.

—MAY SARTON TO MARGARET FOOTE HAWLEY

Noni, dear, thank you for continuing to make me feel that I may
write this kind of epistle to you. It is indeed a saga...
and I'm incapable of writing it to myself, which is of course the main reason
why I am not this minute writing a novel instead of this sort of thing:
I simply have to have someone I love to write to (and for...).

—MFK FISHER TO NORAH KENNEDY BARR

Letters are expectations packaged in an envelope.

—SHANA ALEXANDER

Isn't it nice to write a letter one doesn't have to write? So this is one. I've been walking on the marsh and found a swan sitting in a Saxon grave. This made me think of you. Then I came back and read about Leonardo—Kenneth Clark—good I think: this made me also think of you. And in a minute I must cook some macaroni...

—Virginia Woolf to Vita Sackville-West

Now, I do not despise good letters, indeed, I love them, and if I write one now and then, I am glad of it.

—Katherine Anne Porter to Caroline Gordon

A letter is, as a form of otherworldly communication, less perfect than a dream, but the rules are the same. Neither can be ordered. We dream and write not as *we* want, but as *they* want. A letter *has* to be written: a dream *has* to be seen. (My letters *always* want to be written!)

—Marina Tsvetayeva to Boris Pasternak

I live a solitary life. My gregariousness is letters...

—Donald Hall

Letter writing is the only device for combining solitude with good company.

—Lord Byron

The good thing about not seeing you is that I can write you letters.

—Svetlana Alliluyeva

When the whole world is writing letters, it's easy to lap into the quiet within, tell the story of an hour, keep alive the narrating inner life. To be alone in the presence of one's thought is not a value, only a common practice.

—Vivian Gornick

There is this about letter-writing. I grant it freely. One can gas on *ad infinitum* about the eternal ego without receiving any personal violence in return or any interruption. Thus it is superior to conversation.

—Dawn Powell to Charlotte Johnson

Or don't you like to write letters. I do because it's such a swell way to keep from working and yet feel you've done something.

—Ernest Hemingway

It does me good to write a letter which is not a response to a demand, a gratuitous letter, so to speak, which has accumulated in me like the waters of a reservoir.

—Henry Miller

When I write letters these days, it's to convey an idea,
to express my thanks, my appreciation, my sympathy, or my
congratulations—to construct a piece of writing almost as if
the letter were a polished piece of creative writing.

—Shawn Wong

I never know what will happen when I write a letter.
Certain persons bring out certain things in me.

—Leslie Marmon Silko to James Wright

There is something about the form and occasion of a letter—
the possibility it offers, the chance to be as open and tentative and
uncertain as one likes and also the chance to formulate certain
ideas, very precisely—if one is lucky in one's thoughts.

—James Wright

Letters are above all useful as a means of expressing the ideal self;
and no other method of communication is quite so good for this purpose....
In letters we can reform without practice, beg without humiliation,
snip and shape embarrassing experiences
to the measure of our own desires...

—Elizabeth Hardwick

I used to write long, nutty letters to friends,
freely associating in the after-midnight hours...
Reading or writing that kind of letter
was like going to a party.

—MARVIN BELL

One can use spoken words to reveal one's personal self
to strangers. But written words heighten the privacy of feelings.

—RICHARD RODRIGUEZ

Pondered, shaped, re-read, revised,
considered as written documents in which our words would remain
to honor or to haunt us, letters required us to be more thoughtful than we are
in everyday conversation, often more eloquent, and to picture,
throughout the writing process, the person to whom we were speaking,
so there was a kind of tact and sensitive perception of the receiver,
making letter writing an idiosyncratic and imaginative act.

—ELEANOR WILNER

Letters have to pass two tests before they can be classed as good:
they must express the personality both of the writer and of the recipient.

—E. M. FORSTER

There is no such thing as formal e-mail, any more than there is a formal telephone call. E-mail is quicker than a letter and more efficient than a telephone call for spreading information about your personal life, but paper is still needed to express sympathy, gratitude, and other serious sentiments and announcements.

—JUDITH MARTIN, "MISS MANNERS"

The telephone is a great knee-jerk machine,
but if you really want to tell someone how you feel,
you need the slowness of the letter.
In a society where everything is fast, it's like going out
in the country and looking up at the stars.

—NICK BANTOCK

I have decided that at this stage of my life I am as obviously a letter-writer as other people may be alcoholics or benzedrine-boys. The need to use words and direct them toward a chosen person is almost physically urgent to me, especially in the mornings. I have always liked it.

—MFK FISHER TO HER SISTER NORAH

It is very good now that we are in a letter writing place (not a meeting place) because letters are so much easier than living. One can give one's best.

—MAY SARTON TO JULIETTE HUXLEY

I write to my mother every day, and of course in a daily letter you end up telling everything—stories, dreams, recipes, family, politics and the world. I never read them again. When I sit down and write while thinking about someone, the writing is much easier.

—ISABEL ALLENDE
(WHO HAS WRITTEN TO HER MOTHER
EVERY DAY FOR THIRTY YEARS)

I used to love the feeling of dropping a letter into the box. For several days, the letter-in-transit would hover around the edges of my consciousness. This delay was an intrinsic part of the pleasure of letter writing.

—NOELLE OXENHANDLE

Make a list of 12 people you like, love, admire and don't hear from often enough (or at all). Each month, choose one person and write a letter. E-mails and cards don't count. A letter would make the day of an unknown author whose work you've admired. Make peace with your old college roommate. Good writing is about relationships, so resurrect, enhance, create or feed some of your relationships. Write a letter. Rewrite it. Then send it.

—INKWELL, *WRITER'S DIGEST*

Go to the effort. Invest the time. Write the letter. Make the apology. Take the trip. Purchase the gift. Do it. The seized opportunity renders joy. The neglected brings regret.

—Max L. Lucado

To send a letter is a good way to go somewhere without moving anything but your heart.

—Phyllis Theroux

I have seldom sent a personal email or text message which I have not afterwards, in some degree, regretted. The old-fashioned pen slowed the transition from natural spoken word (and intended meaning) to unnatural script. It gave time for consideration, as did the manual typewriter. Writing involved effort. A word was pondered before being put to paper, packaged and sent through the post. I remember the ancient sandbox calligraphers in Chen Kaige's film, "The Emperor and the Assassin," and became more careful when I handwrote anything. There was poetry as well as prose in those glorious characters. We should treat letters and words with respect.

—Simon Jenkins

ʔOf course I saved your letters ʕ

Letters are like wine;
if they are sound they ripen with keeping.
A man should lay down letters
as he does a cellar of wine.

—SAMUEL BUTLER

I love this part of my life as much as the beginning....
These are the 'yes' years, when there is so much we can
do—see your friends, write letters, read old ones....

—JEAN CHRISTIE LIEN

When the spirits sink too low, the best cordial is
to read over all the letters of one's friends.

—WILLIAM SHENSTONE

I always knew that my father and grandfather loved me,
but among my most cherished possessions are two letters—
one my grandfather wrote to me when I was about eight years old
and another from my father when I was around ten. The realization
that I was so important that this significant adult in my life took
time out of his busy life to write me, just me, a letter was truly
momentous. Hence, I have treasured these letters all my life.

—Horace Deets

I am a letter keeper. And it is indeed fun to take them out after
years of laying around; it brings back memories long forgotten.

—Arthur Ashe

Somehow your letters seem to represent yourself...
and when I look back upon the past, your correspondence stands out
in bold relief as my brightest happiness and seems
to have been actual conversation with you.

—Eldred Simkins to Eliza Trescot

It is giving me so much pleasure to go through these letters
that I'm glad I've been a hoarder. They recall so many
precious things that one forgets otherwise.

—Rachel Carson to Dorothy Freeman

Save my letters, because some day, if I get home,
I may want to relive this part of my life.

—Ms. Lillian Carter to Gloria Carter Span

My Sunday letters [from Paris] were the times I put these
vignettes together, and made my memories concrete and coherent.
Mama has kept these letters for me, in a manila folder
in the top drawer of her Louis XV desk. And whenever I want them,
whenever I want to remember, they are there for me.
For although I addressed them to Mama and Daddy,
they were always written essentially to myself. Mama and Daddy saw Europe
through my eyes, with my perceptions and impressions.
My letters were unselfconscious and utterly honest, for the time and space
between letters made intimacy easier. My parents learned more about me from
a year of letters than they had in nineteen years of personal interaction.

—Lindsay Lankford

A few nights ago I was going through my box of letters,
now overflowing with five years of shared experiences
and good wishes. I began, inevitably, to reread the contents.
I was impressed all over again, as I reread your and Marianne's letters,
with how supportive and loving you were to me in
that period of transition when I left home

—Brooke Jacobson to her daughter, Babette

I had a letter from Elizabeth [Bishop] a day or two ago,
which I'm thinking of having tattooed on me...

—Marianne Moore

[E-mail is impersonal] A letter is something I keep and
cherish, it's something that's of them versus from them, they've
touched the paper and chosen the stationery to send you.

—Sasha Quinton

When I reread them now, the events those letters describe
come rushing back to me with great immediacy.
Paul noticing the brilliant sparkle of autumn light on the dark Seine,
his daily battles with Washington bureaucrats,
the smell of Montmartre at dusk...
In my letters I enthuse over my first taste of toothsome
French duck roasted before an open fire,
on the gossip I'd heard from the vegetable lady
in the Rue de Bourgogne marketplace,
or the latest mischief of our cat Minette,
or the failures and triumphs of our years of cookbook work.
It is remarkable that our family had the foresight to save those
letters—it's almost as if they know Alex and I were going
to sit down and write this book together one day.

—Julia Child, *My Life in France*

As I learn the advantages and value of e-mail,
I cherish some of the old-fashioned ways more and more.
When I get a real letter now from a real friend
written with a real pen and ink, I read it real slow—
several times—and file it away for safe-keeping.

—LINTON WEEKS

That year we wrote seems far away now, yet these letters remain close—
a kind of monument to your generosity, constancy, and compassion during our
time of dangerous wandering. What's missing, of course, is context: your envelopes
stuffed full of clippings, stamps, feathers, sage; your trips to the post office and
mine; the gatekeeper Jiang tearing off the stamps from America in secret;
Dea and who else trying to read over your shoulder; the sudden glance of Chinese
blue aerograms; the tedious delicate tearing open of impossible glue.
But I can let those extras go. The letters still read—a kind
of invisible bridge we created over the Pacific.

—GEORGE VENN TO LOIS BARRY

Above all else we are sensory beings, learning and developing through our five
senses. And I feel a dimension is being lost. For aside from the care and concern
and time it takes to write a letter and mail it, paper has a certain feel, texture,
smell that reaches us from the sender, as well as thoughts conveyed.

It is an older form of communication well worth preserving.
Those who savor time are not so fearful of spending it.

—NANCY WAIT

I have only to sift through these stacks of letters, still neatly folded in their envelopes...and I am immediately transported back—to high school, camp, college, my first apartment and other significant times in my life.... Letters...from friends and relatives all tell a tale and evoke the sender, even decades later, across continents, time, even death.

—Lisa Chipolone Romeo

Letters make the most interesting reading in the world— especially other people's.

—M. Lincoln Schuster

Letters are among the most significant memorial a person can leave behind.

—Johann Wolfgang von Goethe

[The letters of important people are] what makes our history so rich and flavorsome. We have, not just the Declaration of Independence, but what its authors thought while they were making it, which taverns they went to after work, and what vegetables Jefferson planted when he got home. We know, not just the British burned Washington in 1814, but what the weather was like and how many people Dolley Madison was expecting for dinner (forty). Pity the scholar studying the thin dry history of our deskless days, after everyone pressed Delete Message and Empty Trash folder on our E-mail.

—Barbara Holland

I forgot to say that one of the pleasures of reading old
letters is the knowledge that they need no answer.

—GEORGE GORDON, LORD BYRON

Lady Diana Cooper, a famous beauty and acclaimed actress,
kept nearly every letter she received during her long life. Her
letters, filed alphabetically, eventually filled a metal filing
cabinet, a chest of drawers, several trunks and some brass-bound boxes in
the basement of her London home.

...

When President Harry Truman found his wife at the fireplace
disposing of letters he had written to her over the years
he protested, "But think of history!" "I have," she replied.
Fortunately hundreds of Truman's letters remain.

...

Miriam Rothschild wrote to her cousin, Alix de Rothschild,
every day for thirty-five years, about thirteen thousand letters.
Tragically, all of them were destroyed because her cousin feared
that some of them were 'indiscreet.' An incorrigible correspondent, Miriam
described herself: "My friends used to say I was like a motorbicycle roaring
through England and throwing out letters at every hand!"

Letters are the world's unwritten sonnets.

—CHRISTOPHER MORLEY

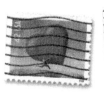

Love letters are the best

Lovers pave the way with letters.

—OVID IN *THE ART OF LETTERS*

The public will always give up its dinner to read love letters.

—GEORGE JEAN NATHAN

When someone writes a letter to a very good friend,
or even more, to his beloved, he puts on his best attire, as well he may.
For in the quiet of his letter, on the tranquil blue paper,
he can express his truest feelings.
The tongue and the spoken word have become so soiled
by their every-day use, they cannot speak out loud the
beauty which the pen can quietly write.

—AUGUST STRINDBERG

A letter does not blush.

—Marcus T. Cicero

It is no pose or deceit if lovers' souls should show up better in their letters to each other than in real life. Nor is the lover false in his love letters. He is not making himself out better than he is: he is becoming better, and in these moments he is better. He is truly himself in such moments, the greatest moments life can bestow on us.

—Alban Berg to Helene Nahowski

If a picture, which is but a mute representation of an object, can give such pleasure, what cannot letters inspire? They have souls; they can speak; they have in them all that force which expresses the transports of the heart; they have all the fire of our passions, they can raise them as much as if the persons themselves were present; they have all the tenderness and the delicacy of speech, and sometimes even a boldness of expression beyond it.

—Heloise to Abelard

More than kisses, letters mingle souls.

—John Donne

I feel like a true lover when I'm writing to you. This letter, which I'm writing with my own hand, with my own pen, in my own penmanship, comes from me and no one else, and is a present of myself to you. It's not typewritten, though I've learned how to type. There's no copy of it, though I suppose I could use a carbon. And it's not a telephone call, which is dead as soon as it's over. No, this is just me, me the way I write, the way my writing is, the way I want to be to you, giving myself to you across a distance, not keeping or retaining any part of it for myself, giving this piece of myself to you totally, and you can tear me up and throw me out, or keep me, and read me today, tomorrow, any time you want until you die.

—ANDY IN A. R. GURNEY'S *LOVE LETTERS*

We write letters because we dare not speak our love in the presence of our loved one. Letters allow us the graceful expression of words we might be unable to stammer out because of nervousness. In a letter, we can deliver a thousand volts of passion, without faltering and without danger.

—MICHELLE LOVRIC,
HOW TO WRITE LOVE LETTERS

The love letter exists on its own, apart from the lover. A literary performance that transforms life, stops time, imagines the future, bridges difference, and privileges a vulnerability usually derided as 'feminine,' the love letter is also an ultimate work of art.

—CATHY N. DAVIDSON,
THE BOOK OF LOVE: WRITERS AND THEIR LOVE LETTERS

Anais Nin wrote to Henry Miller, her lover of many years, "Nothing exists unless it is on paper."

Putting pen to paper
lights more fires than matches ever will.

—Malcolm Forbes

There are no walls in letters.
The words fly out of your heart.

—Anne Sexton

It was nice to get a letter after having so many postal cards. Postal cards are all open and before folks; and to get a letter, sealed and private, is something else. It was like going upstairs after being in company all day with other people, and finding ourselves alone and taking each other in arms and hugging and kissing to our hearts' content.

—James Hague to Mary Ward Hague

If your letters are as long as the bible, they will appear short to me. Only let them be brim full of affection.

—Thomas Jefferson

You can't know how much your letters mean to me...Cooped up here now in a little town far from anyone I know, your letter, full of you and love,... has brought me such pleasure that reading it I sat quiet for several minutes, "smiling all over," as when I hear fine music. Write me some more!"

—WILL TO ARIEL DURANT

What a heavenly morning! All the bells are ringing; the sky is so golden and blue and clear—and before me lies your letter. I send you my first kiss, beloved.

—ROBERT SCHUMANN TO CLARA WIECK

Your two letters, my beloved, lie beside me on the table—
I read them over and over. Oh, Garnet, I feel what you feel—
I understand you completely and fully. Your letters seem to grip me
and hold me... I wake in the morning with your name on my lips—
think of you—mentally write to you all day, and do not end my letter
until as I go to sleep—I say—I am yours. It is not
ended even then—for—happily—I dream.

—KATHERINE MANSFIELD TO GARNET TROWELL

I entered my room and saw your letter on the table. I felt
like falling upon my knees before it. The fact is, if I go on
loving you as I do I shall run the risk of exploding.

—ALBERT JANIN TO VIOLET BLAIR

When Beatrice Campbell asked George Bernard Shaw's permission to publish his love letters, he responded: "No, I refuse to play horse to your Lady Godiva."

...

Asked if she might be willing to make public any of her letters to Ben Reitman, Emma Goldman adamantly refused, saying it would be "like tearing off my clothes."

...

H. L. Mencken and Sara Haardt exchanged more than 700 letters over a seven year period before they overcame their philosophical opposition to matrimony. Their marriage is said to have been an extraordinarily happy one.

...

Victor Hugo's mistress, Juliette Drouet, wrote him more than 20,000 letters during their fifty year relationship.

...

William Wordsworth's sister Dorothy is generally acknowledged as the writer of many of the romantic notes that his wife Mary received from the poet, both before and after their marriage.

...

David Herbert Donald described the love letters of Thomas Wolfe and Aline Bernstein as "something like a duet between a tuba and a piccolo."

It seems like forever since you wrote

To long for certain letters is to be fully human,
and to admit a common humanity.

—W. H. Auden

I am glad you wrote to me.
I thought I had died or something.

—Ann Grey Harvey (Ann Sexton) to another poet

Indeed, I am very uneasy, my love, at receiving no news of you;
write me quickly four pages, pages full of agreeable things
which shall fill my heart with the pleasantest feelings. I hope
before long to crush you in my arms and cover you with a
million kisses burning as though beneath the equator.

—Napoleon Bonaparte to Josephine

Dearest, what have I done that makes you torment me so?
No letter again today, neither by the first mail nor the second.
You do make me suffer! While one written word from you could
make me happy! ...I should like to throw myself bodily on this
letter, so that it cannot be mailed, but it must be mailed.

—FRANZ KAFKA TO FELICE BAUER

You expect, perhaps, that I should accuse you of negligence.
You have not answered my last letter,
and thanks to Heaven,
in the condition I am now in it is a relief to me
that you show so much insensibility
for the passion which I betrayed.
At last, Abelard, you have lost Heloise for ever.
Notwithstanding all the oaths I made
to think of nothing but you,
and to be entertained by nothing but you,
I have banished you from my thoughts, I have forgot you.
...This very moment I receive a letter from you;
I will read it and answer it immediately.
You shall see by my promptitude in writing to you
that you are always dear to me.

—HELOISE TO ABELARD

My dear Katey
Please remember you owe me a letter. I am not going to confirm you in your sins by writing one until I get it. This is merely a note to tell you that I am reading that book of Irish Tales...I have a lot of things to say but will say nothing.

Write to me.

Write to me.

Write to me.

Write to me

till then I am dumb. It is about six weeks since your letter was due. Yours,

—W.B. Yeats to Katherine Tynan

I wish to God, dear sister, that you were as regular in letting me have the pleasure of knowing what passes on your side of the globe, as I am careful in endeavouring to amuse you by the account of all I see that I think you care to hear of. You content yourself with telling me over and over, that the town is very dull: it may possibly be dull to you, when every day does not present you with something new; but for me that am in arrear at least two months' news, all that seems very stale with you would be fresh and sweet here. Pray let me into more particulars, and I will try to awaken your gratitude, by giving you a full and true relation of the novelties of this place...

—Lady Mary Wortley Montagu to the Countess of Mar

It takes two to write a letter as much as it takes two to make a quarrel.

—Elizabeth Drew

I have had four days of complete inertia caused by homesickness and no mail.... nobody loves me, I am forgotten, I hate [her roommate] Mabel's guts, they push me too hard here, no clothes, no food, no nothing, I wish I were dead!

I ran home to lunch, and sat down to cry when I heard footsteps
on the stairs—God! The mailman! Letters from home!

I'm pepped up, everybody loves me, I don't have enough to do, Mabel is real sweet, food is even better than I expected, and life is wonderful.

—Ms. Lillian Carter to Gloria Carter Spann

I long to receive a three page, heart-rending, soppy letter, filled with words carefully chosen and eternal. (OK—I'd be happy with one page—I'm not hard to please.)...Maybe I'm just a hopelessly romantic dreamer, or just downright old-fashioned.

—Bobbie Ann Pimm

Please keep me alive with letters. Write at least once a month. I shall do my best to keep up from this end.

—V.S. Naipul to his sister Kamla

Mail is very eventful to me. Let me hear how you do.

—Flannery O'Connor

In an age like ours, which is not given to letter-writing, we forget what an important part it used to play in people's lives.

–ANATOLE BROYARD

The phone is ringing now and a sullen neighbor is approaching my front door. I might not answer one of them but I better end this letter now. Write to me some time. I miss your letter writer's voice.

—MIKE BERNARD TO SIMONNE DE GLEE

Your trips into the California redwood groves and rocky beaches sound idyllic. Do write, even if it is a message on birch bark written with squid ink.

—PHILIP CARLSON

The U.S. mail is not really about speed. It's not even about certainty. It's about history and mystery and letters of love. It's about the Pony Express. It's about stopping by the student center and finding the perfumed letter slanting sideways in the cubbyhole like a lavender backslash. It's about Dear John, send money, summer camp and sealing wax.

—LINTON WEEKS

I write to you out of turn, and believe I must adopt
the rule of only writing when I am written to, in
hopes that may provoke more frequent letters.

—THOMAS JEFFERSON TO HIS DAUGHTER,
MARTHA JEFFERSON RANDOLPH

She rocked a bit, then said "I 'spose you got one of them
home computers." I said yes, we did. What for? She asked.
I said well, my husband used it for his work, and he did our
finances on there. I used it to write letters...Write letters?
she said. I said yes. She said, You mean you don't write them
on stationery? I said no. She said well pardon me for saying
so, but that's a crying shame. What with the stationery
they got now. She said, I was in town the other day at the
Hallmark, and the stationery they had there, it took my
breath away. Birds and seashells and flowers and cut-lace
edges, some designs so beautiful I felt the tears start. You
know how they do, she said, when you like something so
bad. I said yes. Well, she said, tell me true, wouldn't you
rather get a letter on that kind of paper? I said I guessed
she was right. I didn't want to get into the fact that it
was a rare person who wrote a letter at all anymore.

—ELIZABETH BERG, *THE PULL OF THE MOON*

It's a less than perfect world

It seems a long time since the morning mail
could be called correspondence.

—Jacques Barzun

I miss the days before e-mail when people would send you a letter
via U.S. mail and reasonably expect that a week might pass before you
would respond. And then they certainly wouldn't call you ten minutes
after sending the letter to find out why you hadn't responded yet.

—Carolyn Laub

I would have answered your letter sooner,
but you did not send one.

—Goodman Ace

One serious drawback about letters is that, in order to get them,
one must send some out. When it comes to the mail,
I feel it is better to receive than to give.

—Joseph Epstein

I am a long time answering your letter, my dear Miss Harriet,
but then you must remember that it is an equally long time since I received it—
so that makes us even, and nobody to blame on either side.

—Mark Twain

Most personal correspondence of today consists of letters
the first half of which are given over to an indexed statement
of why the writer hasn't written before, followed by one paragraph
of small talk, with the remainder devoted to reasons why it
is imperative that the letter be brought to a close.

—Robert Benchley

Sometimes I wish there were a computer that I could attach to my
brain that would write down automatically all the letters I wrote to
you in my head. I just wrote you a great one, as I lay on the couch
with my eyes closed...have no idea if I can remember it all...

—Barbara Shulgold to Lynne Sipiora

I just never seemed to have time to pick up a pencil and grab a scrap
of stationery to write anyone anything. Even Santa got short changed.
That's changed since I've made dear friends that are now scattered
from Germany to Seattle, and getting letters from them is like eating
chocolate cheese cake—satisfying, but I don't get to do it very often.

—VERNITA EDIGER

With a regret so deep as to be unfathomable, I am a product
of the telecommunications age and my cupboard of correspondence is bare.

—WALTER CRONKITE

How frail and ephemeral...is the material substance of letters, which
makes their very survival so hazardous. Print has a permanence of its own,
though it may not be much worth preserving, but a letter! Conveyed by
uncertain transportation, over which the sender has no control; committed
to a single individual who may be careless or inappreciative; left to the mercy
of future generations, of families maybe anxious to suppress the past, of
the accidents of removals and house-cleanings, or of mere ignorance. How
often it has been by the veriest chance that they have survived at all.

—ELIZABETH DREW

In our country economy, letter writing is an hors d'oeuvre.
It is no part of the regular routine of the days.

—THOMAS JEFFERSON

To speak critically, I never received more than one or two letters in my life—I wrote this some years ago—that were worth the postage.

—Henry David Thoreau

I find that I really have little to tell you.
I am living such a quiet life, doing the same things
day after day. What shall I write about?

—V.S. Naipul

There is nothing to write about, you say.
Well then, write and let me know just this—that there is nothing
to write about; or tell me in the good old style if you are well.
That's right. I am quite well.

—Pliny the Younger

A man who publishes his letters becomes a nudist—
nothing shields him from the world's gaze except his bare skin.
A writer, writing away, can always fix himself up
to make himself more presentable, but a man who has
written a letter is stuck with it for all time.

—E. B. White

This is a free country. Folks have a right to send me
letters, and I have a right not to read them.

—WILLIAM FAULKNER

There [is] no Rule in the World to be made for writing Letters, but
that of being as near what you speak Face to Face as you can; which is
so great a Truth, that I am of Opinion Writing has lost more Mistresses
than any one Mistake in the whole Legend of Love. For when you
write to a Lady for whom you have a solid and honourable Passion,
the great Idea you have of her, joined to a quick Sense of her Absence,
fills your Mind with a Sort of Tenderness, that gives your Language
too much the Air of Complaint, which is seldom successful.

—RICHARD STEELE

It is well to write love letters. There are certain things for which it is
not easy to ask your mistress face to face, like money for instance.

—HENRI DE REGNIER

If you must reread old love letters, better pick a room without mirrors.

—MIGNON MCLAUGHLIN

A woman's best love letters are always written to the man she is betraying.

—LAWRENCE DURRELL

The talent of writing agreeable letters is peculiarly female.

—Henry Tilney in Jane Austen's *Northanger Abbey*

I wonder if Eve could write letters in Paradise!
But, poor Eve, she had no one to write to—no one to whom
to tell what Eden was, no beloved child to whom her love
traveled through any or all space. Poor Eve!

—Catharine M. Sedgwick

An intention to write never turns into a letter. A letter
must happen to one like a surprise, and one may not know where
in the day there was room for it to come into being. So it is that my daily
intentions have nothing to do with this fulfillment of today.
They were concerned with much that I am now saving up to tell personally.
For the many experiences and impressions are still heaped up in me in such
disorder and chaos that I do not want to touch them.
Like a fisherman who comes home late at night, I can guess
only vaguely at my catch from the burden of the nets
and must wait for the morrow in order to count it
and enjoy it like a new discovery.

—Rainer Maria Rilke to Frieda von Bulow

Now that I'm actually sitting down to write to you,
I don't know what to say. If I question some of your statements,
it might sound as if I were challenging you. If I asked for clarification it would
sound as if I were getting bogged down on petty details.
If I talk about feeling, it might seem that I'm hurt.
If I deny what you ascribed to me, it puts you on a guilt trip.
If I stand on my principles or quote from my heroines or
heroes, it might sound pompous or self-righteous.

Nonetheless, I do have to say a few things...

I know that I love and care for you...and I think you love
and care for me, too. So what more is there to say?

—TO MARION COHEN FROM HER MOTHER

I remind myself of my grandfather, who used to say: 'I shall
write to the man and say Dear Sir:' And after he died they found
his desk full of stacks of writing paper, dated, and beginning
in his flowing hand—Dear Sir—and nothing more.

—SYLVIA TOWNSEND WARNER TO WILLIAM MAXWELL

There are a great many people who really believe in answering letters
the day they are received, just as there are people who go to the movies
at 9 o'clock in the morning; but these people are stunted and queer.

—CHRISTOPHER MORLEY

...My daughter and I have established a new and strong tie;
we engage in a fine and remarkable correspondence,
notable for her ability to say everything that is necessary
in two sentences without punctuation
and my own surprising ability to write that hardest of all things,
a letter to a girl six years old.

—James Thurber to E.B. White

Do not think that you must write to me because I have written to you.
It does not follow at all. You would naturally make so long a speech to me
here in a month as a letter would be. Yet if sometimes it should be perfectly
easy, and pleasant to you, I shall be very glad to have a sentence.

—Henry David Thoreau to ten-year old Ellen Emerson

The present letter is a very long one, simply because
I had no leisure to make it shorter.

—Blaise Pascal

I wish you would ever write a Letter
half as long as I write to you.

—Abigail Adams to John Adams

It was very pleasant to me to get a letter from you the other day.
Perhaps I should have found it pleasanter if I had been able to
decipher it. I don't think that I mastered anything beyond the
date (which I knew) and the signature (which I guessed at).

There's a singular and a perpetual charm in a letter of yours;
it never grows old, it never loses its novelty. One can say to oneself
every morning: There's that letter of Morse's. I haven't read it yet.
I think I'll take another try at it today, and maybe I shall be able in
the course of a few days to make out what he means by those t's that
look like w's and those i's that haven't any eyebrows.

Other letters are read and thrown away and forgotten;
but yours I keep forever–unread.
One of them will last a reasonable man a lifetime.

—Thomas Bailey Aldrich to Edward Sylvester Morse

I wish sometimes you answered some of my letters.
I don't mean point by point, but often I have suddenly remembered
something I have written to you about, and have no idea if you
agreed or disagreed. In the end it is mightily like talking to myself,
only more boring. I have got bored now and must sleep.

—Mary Booker to Richard Hillary

This at least should be a rule through the letter-writing world—
that no angry letter be posted til four and twenty hours
will have elapsed since it was written.

—Anthony Trollope

Somebody just back of you while you are fishing is as bad as someone
looking over your shoulder while you write a letter to your girl.

—Ernest Hemingway

A letter is an unannounced visit, and the postman is the
intermediary of impolite surprises. Every week we ought to have
one hour for receiving letters, and then go and take a bath.

—Friedrich Nietzsche

I do think the art of letter writing will evolve and change because of e-mail...
It may soon feel artificial and old-fashioned to write a certain kind of letter.
But I haven't been sufficiently converted to e-mail yet to imagine a letterless
world. I still have a profound attachment to the three-dimensional.

—Leslie Katz

What a lot we lost when we stopped writing letters.
You can't reread a phone call.

—Liz Carpenter

I don't write letters. I telephone. Most of the people I know do the same thing. On one level, we are products of the phone companies' commercials, telling us how good it is to make our voices heard across the miles. But the real reason we call instead of write is the same reason we are more likely to turn on the television than pick up a book. It is easier. It gets the job done.

—BOB GREENE

To me, the computer has become the symbol of life's changing tempo.

...

Heaven forbid a person should sit down
and simply take the time to sort out her thoughts in a
well written letter on beautiful stationery.

...

... I hope that the art of writing letters of true and deep expressions
of thought, particularly in important and personal
situations, will never go out of style.

—ROBIN INGRAM

The practice and art of writing letters is dying; for most of us it may already be dead. E-mail has taken over. Written communication in our daily lives now is made up of snippets of prose stored on our electronic desktops... Gone, usually, are the long rambling missives about our lives and work; gone is the thoughtful response, re-read many times, gone, too, is a physical entity that we looked forward to when we approached our mailbox, a physical object that—for some of us—has importance beyond the duration of our lives.

—JIM CARMIN

I don't get five, good, genuine personal letters a year.
The time is coming when the letter written with pen and ink
and sent as a personal message from one person to another
will be as much of a rarity as the gold pocket watch
carried on a chain. It's a shame.

—Andy Rooney

My godfather had requested a fountain pen as a present,
as it was something he'd always wanted but never had.
So I went to one of the biggest office supply stores
in New York City and asked one of the sales staff,
a young woman, if they had fountain pens.

Her response was a blank look; then she asked,
"Is that something you drink with?"
I bought him a sweater.

—Patricia Mainardi

We lay aside letters never to read them again, and at
last we destroy them out of discretion, and so disappears
the most beautiful, the most immediate breath of
life, irrecoverable for ourselves and for others.

—Johann Wolfgang von Goethe

Looking forward to your voice on the page

When you write to me, suppose yourself conversing freely
with me, by the fireside. In that case you would naturally mention
the incidents of the day; as where you had been;
whom you had seen, what you thought of them, etc.
Do this in your letters...

—4TH EARL OF CHESTERFIELD TO HIS NATURAL SON, PHILIP STANHOPE

The most valuable letters to and from friends
are not the glib phrases of a play-by-play report,
but the thoughts that are shaping our lives

—TIMOTHY AEPPEL

You don't know a woman until you have received a letter from her.

—ADA LEVERSON

By nature, a letter is a hybrid (part autobiography, part confessional, part report, part journal, part conversation), and a good letter tames the hybrid, even turning it into an art. A good letter is an act of generosity: it uses the voice its writer thinks with, the voice he talks aloud to himself with.

—Raymond Chandler

Your letters were here—one for each of us—when I came in from lunch at Mrs. Lyman's, feeling a bit depressed and lonely...I came down and saw your letter on the hall chair having somehow missed it? & pounced upon it! Don't say it's not a real letter–length means nothing–but "depth" does—some word risen straight up from your heart—that that makes a real message and somehow you attain this almost always—(it can be a gay & light word just as well as a deep thought...it just has to be you, your own self)—So many people seem incapable of conveying the tiniest bit of themselves by letter & that is heartachingly disappointing.

—Eleanor Mabel Sarton to May Sarton

Oh! how I enjoyed it. It was a perfect luxury to read and reread it. I could almost fancy that I heard your sweet voice and could look up and see that 'quiet eye' gazing on me. Why I enjoyed it so very much I really don't know except that it all somehow seemed so like what you used to say when I was near you.

—J. Bolton to Anna Harrison

Is not this the pleasure of corresponding with a friend, where doubt and distrust have no place, and everything is said as it is thought?

—SAMUEL JOHNSON

A letter is a mutual conversation between absent friends, which should be neither unpolished, rough, nor artificial, nor confined to a single topic, nor tediously long. Thus the epistolary form favours simplicity, frankness, humour, and wit.

—DESIDERIUS ERASMUS OF ROTTERDAM

I consider it a good rule for letter-writing to leave unmentioned what the recipient already knows, and instead tell him something new.

—SIGMUND FREUD

In letters I desire clarity and brevity, penetration and grace, wit and gravity.

—SEBASTIANO SALVINI

She [Geraldine Jewbury] was so pleased with your letter. 'My dear,' she said to me, 'how is it that women who don't write books write always so much nicer letters than those who do? I told her—it was, I supposed, because they did not write in the valley of the shadow of their possible future biographer—but wrote what they had to say frankly and naturally...

—JANE CARLYLE TO MARY RUSSELL

...*Especially* in letters put down the thoughts warm and vivid as they present themselves before your fancy. They often gain in vigor what they want in elegance: besides it is good to be uninteresting and even stupid sometimes when we address a friend.

—LORD CHESTERFIELD TO HIS SON

The art of art, the glory of expression and the sunshine of the light of letters, is simplicity.

—WALT WHITMAN

Please give me some good advice in your next letter. I promise not to follow it.

—EDNA ST. VINCENT MILLAY (1892 – 1950), LETTERS

Whenever I allow myself to become too anxious to please the person I am writing to or the person I am writing for, I generally lose balance and spoil everything. The result is bound to be a stilted business. Don't care to please any person but yourself. Only see that you succeed in saying exactly what you want to say without showing off–with utter, brave sincerity–and you will achieve style because you will have been yourself. If in the chase for clarity you have to ignore a rule of grammar, ignore it. If for the sake of euphony you must use a long word, use it. My goodness!

—SEEPERSAD NAIPUL TO V.S. NAIPUL

There are so many things you could write about

If you're regularly in contact with people on the telephone or by e-mail, they're probably up to date on your daily activities, but that doesn't mean they wouldn't love to see a letter from you in their mail box. Instead of reporting recent events, you can look back to remember a funny or important incident, describe a favorite place, recall a notable activity or remarkable person. Everyone likes stories, but opportunities to tell them don't often come up in daily conversations.

When Mary Alice Rose Bishop died at age 92, her obituary included references to her early days in the Frenchtown Valley west of Missoula and the sixty years she lived in Portland, Oregon. She was described as "a great talker and storyteller, but if ever put in the limelight, she was struck dumb. Her Christmas cards (more than 200) became legends for the letters she included telling family stories of the Good Old Days."

A handy audience isn't always available when you're thinking about interesting stories from times past. By sharing those memories in letters, you can enjoy reliving those experiences and—who knows?—your letters could eventually find an honored spot in the family's scrapbooks as well as initiating a "story exchange" with friends.

"Do you remember when we...?" or "For a long time I've been meaning to tell you..." are favorite opening lines for reminiscences, especially because they include your reader in the story. Friends will love being reminded of the good and bad and funny and challenging times you all shared.

Other possible opening lines:

- I've been thinking about how much I loved to...

- If there's one thing I really hated to do when I was a kid it was...

- I really miss the old...

- My favorite place in our family's house was...

- It's amazing that we survived some of the dumb things we did when we were kids. I remember the time we...

- I have to laugh when I think about how proud I was of my first...

- Before I left home I actually thought... was true but now I know...

- Ever since... I've been wondering about...

Here are more ideas. You may already be thinking of better topics:

- Family members that you spent time with, especially the eccentric ones

- Special things about your family's home or a favorite place nearby

- Your name. Did you like it? Why or why not? Did you wish you had another name? What was it?

- The kids you liked the most and the ones you didn't like

- A time that you *really* got into trouble and how you were disciplined.

- Pets or other animals that meant a lot to you

- Going to school, favorite or worst teachers and lessons

- What it was like going to the doctor or the dentist

- Favorite sports, games and toys

- Jobs you had to do—and what you thought about them

- Your best or most-hated clothes

- Your favorite or most-hated foods

- Music you played or listened to

- Holiday celebrations and family traditions

- Money, how you earned it and what it would buy

- Something you really wanted at some time in your life.
  How you managed to get it. What happened to it?

- Automobiles and other kinds of transportation

- What you planned for your life when you first left home

- Some very good or remarkably bad advice someone gave you

- Things about "the good old days" that you miss now,
  or that you're *glad* to miss

- What you are most proud of

- What you wish you hadn't done or had done very differently

- Things that surprise you now because of the way you lived then

We can't expect our friends and families to be fascinated by the routine events of our daily lives, but we can have a wonderful time remembering and writing about some of our most interesting experiences and choosing just the right words to share memories of a world that's uniquely our own.

It is chiefly—perhaps only—in letters that one gets the
mother-of-pearly shimmer inside the oyster of fact.

—Christopher Morley

But wait! There's more!

Sometimes we just need to be reminded of what we know. It's easy to be so comfortable with the details of our lives that we don't recognize how interesting they can be to someone else. The surprising things we pull out of our memories during long lazy conversations are usually sparked by others' comments. When we're flying solo, we sometimes need to fine tune our awareness of topics that will be fun to write about.

I've jotted down a number of quick ideas, mostly generated by alliteration (dreams and desires) or opposing situations (near misses, tough collisions). You've probably heard about adventure travelers who throw a dart at a map or open an atlas at random, then point to a spot that will be the destination for their next trip. In the same spirit, you can turn the page and put your pen or finger somewhere on the page. Good idea? If not, move up or down the list, or—at the least, you may find yourself thinking "Oh... That's silly, but I could write about..." and there you go!

vacations and inspirations

friends and lovers

conquests, creations and calamities

health and happiness

horrors and heroic behavior

dreams and desires

family members and mutual friends

what's old and what's new

issues, ideas, and inventions

wishes, lies and laughs

church and children

food and fun

surprises and satisfactions

habits and hobbies

concerns and compulsions

purchases and promises

routines and recreations

politics and persuasions

changing your life style, changing your mind

looking forward, looking back

going out, staying home

recipes and remedies

common sense and curiosities

plots and plans

near misses, tough collisions

fads and frustrations

achievements and embarrassments

questions and suggestions

lady luck and lessons learned

around the house, around the world

what's working, what isn't

fond memories, interesting dreams

artistic performances and athletic accomplishments

smart moves, dumb decisions

It all depends on the mood of the moment

If you're satisfied and happy with letters as you've always written them, that's truly wonderful. Your lucky friends love your letters and tell you how much they look forward to hearing from you. Please don't think about changing your own charming style. Really. This chapter is not for you.

Some of us, on the other hand, aren't writing letters or are less than satisfied with the letters we write. This might be lingering unease from elementary school lessons that focused on correct salutations and closings, punctuation and spelling. All those rules crowded out the fun of deciding what we wanted to say and how we wanted to say it. Even worse, in school settings—except for the quick notes we scribbled to pass across the aisle—we usually wrote generic letters to make-believe people.

One of the great pleasures in writing letters now is making choices. When you settle down to write with a good friend in your mind's eye, you can be intensely yourself. Think about your mood and situation at that precise moment, sift through your memories, thoughts and experiences to choose the most appealing items to interest the particular person who will soon be receiving your letter. Ideally you'll be smiling as you write, teasing or exaggerating a bit, admiring a phrase that's just popped out on the page. Of course, sometimes serious occasions arise. For those hard times, sensitive and supportive letters are appropriate. In any case, you hope your letter will bring delight or consolation.

If you never try any of the following suggestions, that's just fine. They're modest proposals, reminders that our letters can be as individual as our friendships. We wouldn't select the same gift for every one of our friends, and there's no reason to write the same kinds of letters. Most of the time, we can look forward to being entertaining and lighthearted, even dare to surprise ourselves!

I'm feeling like

Consider the many roles people play in their every day lives: friend, parent, sibling, worker, student, retiree, amateur artist, political observer, community volunteer, wilderness camper, gourmet cook, aspiring athlete, dare devil commuter. Write in the voices of the roles that best reveal your current interests and situation.

Feeling bored or light hearted? Assume a false identity and write in that voice: private detective, interior decorator, representative of a topical magazine requesting an interview, checker at the local market, family pet, yoga instructor. An assumed identity sets the stage for reporting routine events in a new way.

Where I am now

Describe in as much detail as possible where you are at that precise moment. Let your reader see and sense you in that spot, and then ask them for a similar description of their place when they write you back.

Where we were then

Describe in as much detail as possible—colors, shapes, textures, sounds, aromas, feelings—your memories of the place and occasion when you were last together. It will put the reader right there with you, flattered that you remember so clearly. Or write an exaggerated recollection of all the wrong details—that should prompt a reply with a corrected—or even odder—version of events.

Tell me about it

Ask questions, serious or not: Where in the world were you last Halloween? Was your costume as stunning as usual? Surely the newspaper accounts were exaggerated? ☜ In your wildest dreams, did you ever imagine we might become PTA presidents? stock brokers? triathalon competitors? fashion consultants? food bank volunteers? world travelers? ☜ Where do you think we'll be ten years from now? I'm wondering if my job might put me in... or if I'll be tied down with... or savoring the delights of... ☜ Are you still... or pursuing that... we used to talk about?

You'll never believe this

Begin with a lie—a huge whopper: "Ever since we took up swimming with sharks …decided to move to Uruguay …donated our lifetime collection of Readers' Digests to the Smithsonian …began to eat only organically grown raw food…

The truth, they say, will set you free, but telling a big fib may get you started— who knows what will follow?

All the news that's fit to print

Think of your letters as parts of mini-newspapers. Most papers have sections for news, features, business, sports, social announcements, crime reports and classified ads. Our lives tend to fall within (or outside of) those classifications. If your letter is mostly sports page or mostly society section, you can adopt or exaggerate that vocabulary and writing style. Are you being the *Wall Street Journal* or the *Enquirer*?

The shape of things

There's no rule that letters must be written in paragraphs. Consider lists— top ten reasons for …or use contrasting lists of best things and worst things going on at the moment. Just drawing a line down the middle of the page and numbering the items may spark your imagination. You could even list all the things you decided against writing about. If all has been going exceptionally well—or badly—list several possible titles for your forthcoming autobiography with brief explanations based on those titles.

There's also no rule that letters must be written on stationery. You can use odd pieces of paper, concert flyers, yard sale notices, takeout menus, lost dog posters, or gift wrapping paper. Is it one of those days when you feel like cutting out paper dolls? OK—write notes on each one—fold them up and think about your friend unfolding your "letter." Or cut out geometric shapes, free-form blobs that make small spaces for writing.

One letter writer, determined to go beyond the ordinary, writes in small letters on adding machine tape which she carefully threads through the film spools of old cameras to which she attaches the address labels. A wealth of similarly unusual efforts is outlined on the MailArt web site.

Ignoring the calendar

(Is this Nobel Prize worthy?) An easy way to improve annual holiday letters is to write them at another time entirely: national letter writing month in April, solstices, equinoxes, anniversaries, birthdays, whenever you feel like taking stock of your life and communicating with friends. Outside the frenzy of the holidays, there will be more leisure to individualize letters and more time for friends to read them and—perhaps—even time to answer.

Making a promise

Mail a postcard with a note saying a letter's on the way. The postcard is easy to write, and as a best-selling author urges: "Write it down, make it happen." Once that card is in the mail, you've promised that a letter will follow. If you use small stationery, it's easy to fill a page, and once you've filled one page, maybe you'll want to write more. "Blank" note cards provide illustrations for almost every mood and occasion to complement the letter you'll slip inside.

Writing can be typing

If your handwriting is legible, let your friends enjoy it. If you prefer typing, especially if typing lets you write longer letters, do that. In either case, by the time you've chosen paper, pen or font, words on the page, envelopes, enclosures and stamps, your letter will be uniquely and personally your own.

Another suggestion about typing: As you read your e-mail, if you discover that you've written an especially long and interesting reply, instead of clicking 'Send,' think about copying your 'e-mail' letter to your word processing program, print it using an interesting font like Palatino, Book Antiqua, or Garamond (italicized), put it in an envelope and mail it. Your genuine printed letter in a hand-addressed envelope will definitely get more attention than one that's sent on-line.

The gift of a letter

For the special people on your gift list: A personal letter is a unique gift that will always fit and never go out of style. A letter to a long-time friend or cherished family member, written with obvious care, describing happy memories or recounting specific appreciations, will be especially valued as a lasting reminder of your affection.

The envelope please

The pleasure of opening an envelope and unfolding the pages of a letter is even more delightful when we find 'something more'—a small addition tucked in the last fold. (For some of us, that's a reminder of years of happily searching for tiny prizes in the bottom of Cracker Jack and cereal boxes or finding dollar bills in birthday cards.)

Small enclosures let us share the rich texture of a new fabric swatch, the miraculous silky geometry of a bird's feather, the sweet aroma of rose petals or the sharp tang of a sprig of sagebrush. These tiny bits of our real-life encounters could never be e-mailed—even with the best scanner. That's why it's so much fun to include them. And even though it's easy to e-mail digital photos, it's thoughtful to send prints that are ready to share or display, especially since some of us have a tenuous relationship with our computers' color printers.

Occasionally the desire to send a special item will be the reason for a letter. Or, as you're writing, just the right addition may occur to you, a perfect choice to match a friend's interests, something to make them smile or puzzle over. Common sense will guide your decisions. The US Postal Service has rules about objects that interfere with stamp cancellation machinery. When in doubt, call 1-800-ASK USPS or check the USPS Homepage on line.

- Photographs of friends and family (Don't send the whole batch at once. Save a few for next time.)
- Photographs of places, pets and projects—everything from mountains climbed to picket fences painted
- Clippings and photo-copies from magazines and newspapers
- Cartoons
- Travel brochures
- Maps with notations about trips you've taken
- Theater and concert programs
- Fortune from a Chinese fortune cookie
- Floor plans of your house or apartment
- Fabric swatches, paint chips or samples of wallpaper
- Bird feathers, dried flowers or leaves
- Recommended recipes
- Locks of a baby's or puppy's hair
- A snip of your new hair color
- College course descriptions
- Ads for something you're thinking about buying or doing (a car, a two-week cruise)
- A new pet's paw print
- A song or poem or story you've written
- Anything that will fit in an envelope—or you can include a note about something silly that won't fit, but you'd like to include (like the guy next door who practices the tuba at 6:00 every morning)

Wise words from the Grand Master

Lewis Carroll (Charles Dodgson) proposed that "The proper definition of man is an animal that writes letters." He wrote and received more than 100,000 letters in the last 37 years of his life. That's 7 or 8 letters a day, every day, for 37 years! At some point in his extended letter writing career, he published a small (4"x3") pamphlet entitled "Eight or Nine Wise Words about Letter-Writing." (His 'wise words' actually numbered closer to 3,500.) His experience as a letter writer qualifies him as a Grand Master of Correspondence. Here's a mini-summary of his rules:

➻ Obtain a stamp case and keep an assortment of stamps available at all times.

➻ To answer a letter, first reread it, then check the address, then address and stamp the envelope before starting the letter. (But never address two envelopes at once; that could lead to inserting the wrong letter in the wrong envelope.) Put your own address on the top of the first sheet and the date in full (not "Tuesday," for example).

◦◦ Write legibly.

◦◦ Don't fill more than a page and a half with apologies for not having written sooner. The best subject to begin with is your friend's last letter. Answer his questions, make appropriate remarks, then start with what you want to say yourself.

◦◦ In controversial correspondence, don't repeat yourself.

◦◦ If you have written a letter that might possibly irritate your friend, put it aside until the next day. Then read it over as if it were addressed to yourself.

◦◦ If your friend has made a severe remark, either leave it unnoticed or respond with a distinctly less severe reply, and don't try to have the last word.

◦◦ If you write in jest, apparently criticizing your friend, exaggerate enough to make the joke obvious.

◦◦ When you say you are enclosing something in a letter, put it in the envelope at that moment; otherwise you may forget to include it.

◦◦ When you get to the end of the note sheet and still have more to say, take another whole piece of paper rather than crowding your last remarks between the lines of the first page.

✒ If you doubt what closing phrase is appropriate, check your correspondent's letter and use an ending that is at least as friendly as his.

✒ A postscript is a very fine invention, but it is not meant to contain the main point of the letter; it is intended to address a minor point you don't want to make a fuss about.

✒ When you've finished your letter, read it through carefully and put in any important small words (like "not") that may have been omitted.

✒ Do not fasten the envelope until just before you mail it; otherwise you may have to open it in order to add something you forgot to say.

✒ On the way to mail a letter, carry it in your hand. If you put it in your bag or pocket, you may forget to mail it.

It's surprising how well Carroll's sensible rules, written more than a hundred years ago, have withstood the test of time.

In 1998, Lee Mingwei created The Letter-Writing Project, an art installation at the Whitney Museum of Art that encouraged visitors "to write letters that we have always intended to write, but have never made the time to compose." They were invited to think about insight, forgiveness and gratitude, but were free to write on any topic. As he said,

> "At a time when communication is everywhere, it is almost losing its meaning. E-mail can be sent instantaneously, but it's not a contemplative kind of experience, it's not a sensual kind of experience."

At Mingwei's installation, which has since traveled to Australia, Korea and Japan, paper and envelopes were provided at three beautifully crafted booths made of glass and wood: one designed for sitting, one for standing, one for kneeling. The letters composed at the booths could either be sealed and addressed to be mailed by museum staff, or left open to be read. Mingwei collected the letters that were left open. He has thousands of them, most of which he has not read because "it was just too much of an emotional experience."

Remarkable History of Mail Delivery

1653

To support his subjects' interest in letter writing, Louis XIV gave
M. Jean-Jacques Renouard de Villayer, a stationer, permission to
put mail boxes on the street corners of Paris. M. Villayer guaranteed
delivery of letters placed in special envelopes bearing a receipt of
purchase from his stores. Unfortunately this first effort to create
a democratic postal system failed because vandals, perhaps rival
stationers, dumped trash and even live rodents in the mail boxes.

1673

When the American colonies started mail service,
the 260 mile trip from Boston to New York took two weeks on
horseback. Mail carriers were expected to mark the route by
blazing trees as well as looking for escaped slaves and deserters.

1673
When 50 cents a day was a living wage
in the American colonies, it cost $3.50, a week's wages,
to send a letter from New York to Philadelphia.

1737
Benjamin Franklin organized the first American Postal Service.

1775
The American colonies appointed Benjamin Franklin
as the first Postmaster General. This appointment marked the birth
of the Postal Department, the 2nd oldest federal agency in U.S.

1794
Although most people continued to collect their mail at the
nearest post office, home delivery became available at the cost of
two cents extra in postage for each letter. Payment of postage fell
to the one receiving the mail on a cash-on-delivery (COD) basis.

1799
U. S. Congress passed a law authorizing the
death penalty for mail robbery.

1830

Rowland Hill invented the gummed postage stamp in England,
which allowed the sender (rather than the recipient)
to pay the postage for mailing a letter. This began
the British Penny Postal System which, over the next
three decades, was adopted all over the world.

1837

First British mail-sorting railway car
("Flying Service") was put into service.

1857

Perforated postage stamps were introduced.

1860

The Pony Express first delivered mail overland across America.
Even though the Pony Express lasted only eighteen months,
(April 1860-October 1861) the heroic business of delivering
mail from coast to coast in a scant ten days ($5 per half-ounce)
is a favorite part of the romantic epic of westward expansion.

~

Advertisement for Pony Express Riders:
"Wanted: Young, skinny, wiry fellows not over 18,
must be expert riders, willing to risk death daily.
Orphans preferred."

1861

On October 26, the transcontinental telegraph line was completed.
Thus ended the Pony Express. In the following decades,
the U. S. Postal Service experimented with using camels,
reindeer, dog teams and underground pneumatic tubes
in efforts to deliver the mail more efficiently.

1863

Free home delivery was initiated in American towns
so relatives wouldn't have to read Civil War death notices
from the War Department at the Post Office.
Before that time, women picked up mail at the
Ladies' Window of the local post office.

1864

First U.S. railway mail-sorting cars were put into service.

1893

First commemorative stamp was issued
for the Chicago World's Fair.

1896

Rural Free Delivery was initiated.

1913
Parcel Post was provided for mailing small packages.

1914
Before the practice was banned, a mother shipped her baby from Stillwell to South Bend, Indiana to its father who had won custody in an acrimonious divorce. For 17 cents, under the watchful eye of postal employees, the baby traveled in a container marked "Live Baby."

~

The same year the parents of four-year old May Pierstroff mailed her from her home in Grangeville, Idaho to her grandparents in another part of the state. May rode in the mail car with 53 cents in postage stamps affixed to her coat, the going rate for shipping chickens.

1916
An entire bank was mailed parcel post from Salt Lake City to Vernal, California. Its 80,000 bricks were shipped in 50 pound lots, one ton at a time. Because of the physical strain on postal employees and railroad workers, the postmaster then ordered a single shipper could post no more than 200 pounds a day.

1918
Regular airmail service was organized for the United States.

1920

On September 8, the last transcontinental segment for airmail delivery was established from Omaha to San Francisco.

1921

For the first time, mail was flown day and night across the entire continent from New York to San Francisco.

1959

On June 8 the USPS reported the successful launch of a rocket carrying 3,000 first class letters from a submarine in the Atlantic Ocean to an airbase in Florida.

1963

Zip codes were introduced.

1982

Twelve million "love" stamps were sold in New York City in three days.

1995

The amount of e-mail delivered in the United States surpassed the amount of mail, printed on paper, delivered by the U.S. Postal Service.

The Smithsonian Postal Museum contains 16 million stamps, the largest collection of its kind in the world.

...

Chris Bohjalian heard that an acquaintance from college he hadn't seen in eight years was attending Middlebury's Bread Loaf School of English in Ripton and house-sitting somewhere in Bristol. He thought it would be nice to catch up and sent him a letter with his name and the most precise address he could come up with:

Aspiring Writer

House-Sitting Somewhere

Bristol, VT 05443

His friend received the letter the very next day, and ever since Bohjalian has marveled at the mysterious power of the U.S. Postal Service Bristol Branch.

...

The familiar quotation inscribed on the post office building in New York City—"Neither snow nor rain nor heat nor gloom of night stays these couriers from the swift completion of their appointed rounds"—was never, as many believe, the official motto of the USPS. Adapted from the writings of the Greek historian Herodotus (5th c. B.C), the words nonetheless suggest the monumental efforts to move the mail in the United States since the establishment of the Post Office Department by the Second Continental Congress in 1775.

The word that is heard perishes,
but the letter that is written remains.

—Proverb

Favorite Collections of Published Letters

I've always loved letters. I have boxes of them and so do thousands of other people. Besides serving as a marvelous resource for historians and biographers, many published volumes of collected letters are as interesting and compelling as the best fiction.

It's fun to read other people's mail. Because they're just chatting on paper, famous people's personal letters are usually more relaxed than their public writing. Depending on the correspondents, it's like enjoying the very best conversation without having to participate. You're settled down in a comfortable chair in the corner, enjoying a cool drink, observing the lively interactions of intelligent people with no obligation to enter the conversation, something like watching *My Dinner with Andre*.

Browsing the titles of letter books might be compared to taking a Rorschach test. It's a quick way to define your interests. Are you intrigued by Gineva King's collected letters (now at Princeton) because they provided models for the idealized debutantes in Scott Fitzgerald's novels? Do you wonder about the volume entitled *Hello My Big Big Honey: Love Letters to Bangkok Bar Girls*? Are you touched by collections of letters written home by those serving in virtually every war? How about spending an evening with the love letters of Ron and Nancy Reagan? Or would you be more interested in reading letters written by outraged consumers to major corporations? No doubt about it. There's great pleasure in letters and the variety is infinite.

Many of my favorite books include both sides of the letter exchange. That's the essence and delight of their correspondence, knowing that their writing partner (co-respondent) likes them, appreciates their situation and is eager to hear from them.

Three of my favorite collections are letters written by women who are not famous at all. They prove that you don't have to be a published author to write witty, sensitive, appealing letters.

Letters as Life Lines

Dear Exile: The True Story of Two Friends Separated (for a Year) by an Ocean, Hilary Liftin, Kate Montgomery. Vintage, 1999.

Kate Montgomery writes good natured reports of their challenges in a third world culture as she and her husband experience difficult Peace Corps assignments in rural Kenya while young Hilary Liftin, her college roommate, responds with tales of urban adventures including job expectations, apartment hunting and failed romance in New York City.

The Garden Letters, Elspeth Bradbury & Judy Maddox. Polestar, 1995.

Elspeth and Judy, neighbors who share a passion for gardening, are separated when the Bradburys move from the extremes of New Brunswick's frigid, dry climate to warmer and wetter British Columbia. These gardening friends write frequently, reporting on the particular challenges of their different climate zones and social environments. Their chatty letters include details of their daily lives, news of small victories and wry accounts of occasional disasters.

Dear Barbara, Dear Lynne: The True Story of Two Women in Search of Motherhood, Barbara Shulgold and Lynne Sipiora, Addison-Wesley, 1992

These letters cover three years of yearning, expectation, regret and fulfill-ment as Barbara and Lynne exchange reports of each family's attempts to adopt a child. Although they have never met, these two women could not have been closer or more sensitive to each other's hopes and disappointments if they had been raised as twins.

Continuing Conversations

My favorites among the collections of published writers' works capture their best conversational voices. Their letters are written in the same unpreten-tious, everyday language any educated person could use. Again, here both correspondents' letters are provided:

The Elements of Lavishness, Letters of Sylvia Townsend Warner and William Maxwell, 1938-1978, Michael Steinman, ed. Counterpoint Press, 2000.

Sylvia Townsend Warner, a young British short story writer living in London begins a professional correspondence with William Maxwell, then a novice editor at the *New Yorker*. They exchange more than 1300 letters over a 40 year period. Michael Steinman selects those letters that best reveal the author's and the editor's appreciation for each other's friendship as well as providing small tales, well told, about the world outside their literary lives.

Glad Tidings, A Friendship in Letters: The Correspondence of John Cheever and John D. Weaver, 1945-1982. Harper Collins, 1993.

These letters, usually short, are obviously quick reports of the moment. They continue a friendship between two notable American writers, formed during their Army service in Queens, N.Y. during WW II. "If I can laugh, I can live," was one of Cheever's last journal entries. These usually light hearted and occasionally serious exchanges connected the Cheevers' home in New England with the Weavers' sunny retreat in Hollywood Hills, California. As the title suggests, experiences and appreciations flew back and forth through their letters, maintaining a close friendship despite the miles that separated them.

Will and Ariel Durant: A Dual Autobiography. Simon and Schuster, 1977.

More than an autobiography, this is the story of a life-long friendship and romance in letters. Ariel, child of impoverished Russian refugees, fell in love with her teacher, Will Durant, when she was only fourteen. They married a year later in 1913, beginning a remarkably intellectual and passionate relationship that involved, among many other projects, their authorship of the eleven-volume *Story of Civilization.* Their letters cover family affairs, social and political issues, friends and recreation, food preferences, demanding writing projects and lecture schedules, discussions of the world's great philosophers and historical figures and always, their abiding love for each other.

Lives in Letters

Like most of the letter collections I've listed, these books are hard to put down. Here we find famous people enjoying the camaraderie provided by spontaneously conversing on paper.

M.F.K. Fisher, Correspondence 1929-1991: A Life in Letters, Norah K. Barr, Marsha Moran and Patrick Moran, eds. Counterpoint Press, 1997.

Beginning with her marriage to Alfred Fisher and three idyllic years living in southern France, Fisher's letters recount a life rich with appreciation for the pleasures of the culinary arts, interesting friends and natural landscapes, where virtually any day's encounters become stories worth telling in letters that reveal an unfailing gift for discerning the unusual in the ordinary.

Steinbeck: A Life in Letters, Elaine Steinbeck and Robert Wallston, eds. Penguin, April 1989.

A huge, carefully edited collection with commentaries by Steinbeck's widow, Elaine. Throughout his lifetime, Steinbeck wrote to his family and cherished friends about his thoughts and feelings as much as about his activities. He was honest, sensitive and unpretentious, obviously delighting in recording bits of his life as he wrote to a number of close friends. As one reviewer remarked, "If you appreciate the art of letter writing, you'll be delighted with this collection."

Congenial Spirits: Selected Letters of Virginia Woolf, Banks, Joan Trautman, eds., Random House, Harvest Books, 1991.

In this vast collection, drawn from six volumes of her letters, Woolf's letters reveal an inventive and spirited correspondent who shifts from reports of daily domestic life to gossip about her writing colleagues to serious discourses on women's rights, women writers and the political issues of the day. If she had never written a novel, Woolf's appealing correspondence would undoubtedly have brought her deserved fame as a fine writer.

Letters of E.B. White, Dorothy Lobrano Guth, ed. Harper and Row, 1976, revised edition, Martha White, ed. 2006.

E.B. White's letters are a chronicle of his three great loves: his family, *The New Yorker* and his farm in Maine. One of America's preeminent authors, his letters to friends—other notable and sophisticated writers—are witty, wise and brilliantly conversational. I keep Burton Bernstein's *A Biography of James Thurber* on the shelf next to the *Letters of E.B. White*, hoping that a magic synchronicity will one day create a collection of Thurber's and White's letters to each other.

Situational Letters

84 Charing Cross Road, Helene Hanff Avon, 1994

This beloved small classic has been adapted for both film and stage. Hanff, a self-described "poor writer" first corresponds with Marks and Company, a London antiquarian book store in 1949. During more than twenty years, her search for affordable copies of classic texts blossoms into a correspondence friendship with the bookstore manager who is disarmed by her breezy Americanisms, generosity of spirit and love for books.

Letters to Jenny, Piers Anthony with Alan Riggs, Smithmark Publishers, 1993.

At her mother's request, Anthony—a well known writer of popular science fiction and fantasy—writes long weekly letters to Jenny, a twelve-year-old fan of his Xanth fantasy series, who is hospitalized with serious injuries after being struck by a drunk driver. Read aloud, Anthony's weekly letters help to penetrate Jenny's coma and then provide needed moral support during her arduous year-long recovery. His detailed accounts of random events of interest to him as well as descriptions of daily life on his family's rural acreage in Florida are remarkable models of the best kind of interesting, collegial letters to young people.

All in the Family

Performing Motherhood: The Sévigné Correspondence, University Press of New England, 1991.

Mme de Sévigné's letters were primarily addressed to her married daughter to whom she wrote at least twice a week between 1671 and 1696 unless they were together. Because Mme Sévigné's experiences encompassed relations with the Court of Louis XIV as well as daily life in Paris, her letters deliver a fascinating historical perspective. As was the custom in the 17th century France, her letters were often circulated among friends and family and became generally admired as works of epistolary art, combining an easy and entertaining style with an elegance of descriptive detail and observation.

Letters/Mary Wortley Montagu, Introduction by Clare Brant. Alfred A. Knopf, 1992.

Following the tradition of Madame Sévigné, Lady Mary Wortley Montagu is regarded as one of the greatest letter writers in the English language. She was erudite and intellectually curious in a time when formal education was customarily denied to women. Her letters, most to her sister and her daughter, often contain incisive reports of her foreign travels with especially astute appraisals of the social customs she observed. Early in the 18th century, when letter writing had been elevated to an art form, Lady Mary's letters were notable for their style and grace.

Visual Delights

Consider the sybaritic delights of curling up for an evening with Nick Bantock's exquisite *Griffin & Sabine* series. The three books contain richly illustrated cards and envelopes from which the curious reader may extract and read intimate letters between two geographically separated and emotionally elusive individuals. Their correspondence spans continents and their wavering commitments. Bantock's artwork perfectly complements their mysterious relationship. Griffin & Sabine's correspondence is "rediscovered," and published in *The Gryphon* in 2001 and *Alexandria* in 2002.

Bantock's books were inspired, he says, by trips to his local post office where, with envy, he watched another man removing letters with exotic stamps from his post office box. His desire for intriguing correspondence triggered the creation of Griffin and Sabine's beautiful cards and letters for all of us who yearn for fascinating letters to enjoy.

Surprising Suggestions

It may seem oxymoronic to send a letter lover to the internet. Not so. These web sites are exceptional. The best is Wendy Russ's *Letters, Letter-writing and other Intimate Discourse*. It can be easily accessed on line by searching "Wendy Russ: Letters." Clearly a labor of love, this charming site contains a vast array of interesting possibilities with links to more than a dozen letter-related topics from Fictional Letters to Civil War Letters to Pen Pal links and the History & Culture of Letter Writing.

Another letters web site, *The Modern Letter Project*, at this writing is 'on hiatus' but may return soon. In the meantime, the monthly archives are well worth visiting.

For pure visual pleasure, visit *The Graceful Envelope Contest*, sponsored by the Washington Calligraphic Guild. It's available at a link from Wendy Russ's letter site or the National Postal Museum's site or by searching "Graceful Envelope Contest." To see dozens of marvelously creative approaches to addressing envelopes, click on "view past contest winners."

Finding Published Letter Collections

Some of the books I've mentioned are still available as new, while others are tucked away in used book stores—what better place to spend a rainy afternoon? Check out your local new and used bookstores where you may find them and fairly recent collections like the *Selected Letters of Martha Gellhorn* (what a life she lived!) and Julia Child's engaging memoir, *My Life in France*, based on the letters Julia and her husband Paul wrote to friends and relatives in the States as Julia was developing her lifelong love affair with France and French cooking.

A few years ago when I was in Powell's main store in Portland, I asked a clerk to check on letter collections for me. The list was so long it crashed the store's computer for almost ten minutes while long lines of customers waited, mostly patiently, to purchase their books. As we waited, the store clerk recommended *Dear Exile*, which as you know, became one of my favorite letter books.

Of course public libraries qualify as one of the world's great bargains. Browsing the on-shelf collections provides unexpected treasures, and most libraries also offer extensive inter-library loan services. University library cards are usually available for a token fee. Their on-line catalogs connect to major university collections, a life-time of reading for interested researchers.

If you're interested in exploring the vast world of published letters, without leaving home you can easily travel great distances through heavily populated territory on the internet. Yesterday my search brought up titles for 549 anthologies of letters at Powells.com. When I log on to Amazon. com's listing of books about letters, I feel like Alice swirling down the rabbit hole to land in front of the longest brightest display one can imagine. Today there are 769,761 letter books listed; tomorrow there will probably be more. Of course that includes books about letters of the alphabet, and a fair number of books about writing business letters and so forth, but there are hundreds and thousands of letter collections. A review of new letter collections published in 2008 includes the letters of Noel Coward, the six Mitford sisters, Graham Greene and Vincent Van Gogh as well as *Women's Letters: America from the Revolutionary War to the Present*, *Letters of the Century*, and *Love Letters of Great Men*. That's a partial listing. We surely have been writing and reading and saving letters for a long time, and there's no point in stopping now!

There are certain people whom one feels almost inclined to urge
to hurry up and die so that their letters can be published.

— CHRISTOPHER MORLEY

Looking Ahead

There's a quiet delight in reading published collections of letters, much like being an unobtrusive but welcome guest, happily listening to articulate friends as they chat about ideas and the news of their lives. Over the years as I enjoyed this pleasant occupation, I started marking the parts of letters that struck me as being particularly entertaining or thoughtful or appropriate to the occasion. From that pastime, *Delicious Conversations: The Easy Art of Writing to Family, Friends and Lovers* has grown.

Just as ardent gardeners pour over gardening books, enjoying thoughts of creating a leafy bower in the back yard, and committed cooks skim through new recipe books in search of culinary inspiration, letter writers profit from observing the craft of those whose letters are models of charming conversations on paper. It's intriguing to see that published authors write in different voices to different friends and that their writing is almost always more relaxed than in their formal published works. Obviously a desire to connect and a willingness to share are more important to these accomplished writers than a need to impress.

Delicious Conversations is organized by the occasions that cover most of the reasons we write to each other:

Personal Letters with Your Personality
Talking on paper

Travel Letters
Becoming a "foreign correspondent"

Love Letters
Sharing amorous messages with your beloved

Thank You Letters
Expressing gratitude for gifts and favors

Condolences and Congratulations
Sending words of comfort and words of joy

Serious Letters
Stating difficult but necessary opinions

Letters to Children
Building bridges to last a lifetime

Story Letters
Telling tales of recent events or happy memories

Holiday Greetings
Making annual missives appealing

One of the delights of browsing these selections is thinking "I could do that." And so you can.

Excerpts from letters by the following writers are included. Their voices reflect their shifting moods and relationships—from light-hearted to serious, patient to exasperated, down-to-earth to philosophical.

Albert Einstein
Alexander Woolcott
Algernon Swinburne
Anais Nin
Ann Morrow Lindbergh
Ann Sexton
Barbara Holland
Barbara Shulgold
Beatrix Potter
Charles Dodgson
Morley, Christopher
Delmore Schwartz
Dorothy Thompson
Dylan Thomas
E. B. White
Earl of Chesterfield
Edward Dickinson
Elizabeth Bishop
Elizabeth Blackwell
Elspeth Bradbury
Emily Eden
Evelyn Waugh
F. Scott Fitzgerald
Flannery O'Connor
Franz Kafka
Freya Stark
Frieda Kahlo
George Bernard Shaw
Georgiana, Duchess of Devonshire
Geraldine Endsor Jewsbury
Gertrude Applegate
Gustave Flaubert

Hannah Arendt
Harry Truman
Hart Crane
Henry David Thoreau
Horace Deets
Isa Kogan
Isabel Burton
James Thurber
James Wright
Jane Austen
Jane Carlyle
Janet Flanner
John Cheever
John O'Hara
John Steinbeck
Joseph Conrad
Judy Maddocks
Julie Gilliss
Juliette Drouet
Kate Montgomery
Katherine Mansfield
Kenneth Koch
Lady Diana Cooper
Lady Mary Wortley Montagu
Lady Randolph Spencer-Churchill
Libby Beaman
Lillian Smith
Lydia Kirk
Lynne Sipiora
Mark Twain
Mary McCarthy
Matthew Arnold

May Sarton
Michael Faraday
Miss Lilian Carter
MKF Fisher
Mme de Sévigné
Napoleon Bonaparte
Nathaniel Hawthorne
Nick Bantock
Ogden Nash
Paul Lawrence Dunbar
Piers Anthony
Rainier Marie Rilke
Richard Halliburton
Richard Steele
Robert Schumann
Rudyard Kipling
S.J. Perelman

Sarah Bernhardt
Shawn Wong
Shizue Iwatsuki
Simone de Beauvoir
Sir Harold Nicholson
Tennessee Williams
Thomas Bailey Aldrich
Thomas Carlyle
V.S. Naipul
Violet Coward
Virginia Woolf
Vita Sackville-West
W.B. Yeats
Will Durant
William Carlos Williams
Wolfgang Amadeus Mozart
Zelda Fitzgerald

Additionally, there are approximately forty passages from letters written by my friends and family. They're proof positive that one need not be famous or published to write appealing letters on a variety of topics.

Recently a new book of selected letters was hailed as a product of "the golden age of correspondence, now sadly vanishing." It would be tragic if we were actually to lose the lasting pleasure of these delicious conversations on paper. I urge you to explore and enjoy *Delicious Conversations*. If, as you read, you're already thinking of the first person you plan to write to, there may be a renaissance of the golden age of correspondence.

Delicious Conversations: The Easy Art of Writing to Family, Friends and Lovers
Please Google my blog for the 2010 publication date at blog.pleasureofletters.com
or write: Best Letters Press, PO Box 566, La Grande, OR 97850

Dear Reader,

Wouldn't it be intriguing to read a collection of the best letters we've all made a point of saving? Not "letters of a nation" or "the best letters of the century," but personal letters we've enjoyed or valued so much that we'd never think of throwing them away? They could be recent or old, long or short, funny, poignant, informative, outraged, loving, satiric or historically interesting.

If you have one or more wonderful letters that you believe would stand on their own in a letter collection, I hope you'll send them to me. I'm interested in personal letters that speak with an individual voice, sparkle with specific details, tell stories, inform and entertain—the kinds of letters my letter-loving friend Mary would call "keepers."

One of my prized possessions was a letter written by my grandfather to my grandmother in 1910. Unfortunately it was lost when our house burned in a forest fire. In that letter, he narrated the process of using coarse black thread to sew a significant portion of his nose on after a stove pipe he was installing in their remote summer home had fallen, nearly severing his nose from his face. I treasured that letter because he described the event with such ironic good humor, exaggerating his clumsiness as a handyman while boasting of his dexterity as an amateur surgeon.

I'd like to see a copy of the disgruntled letter a student told me he had written to his optometrist about less-than-satisfactory new glasses. Robert said he'd written that for $185, he should have been able to discover new galaxies with those glasses, but as it was, he was having trouble seeing the stop signs at intersections.

As you probably know, penmanship has not been a priority in public education for some time. For clarity, I'll need a typed version of hand-written letters along with a photo copy of the originals. Please include a brief introductory note—no more than 100 words—explaining the context of the letter, as well as the date, the name of the person who wrote the letter and the name of the person to whom it was written.

Don't send your original copy of a letter. I'll assume all submissions are photocopies. Of course include your name, address, and telephone number. I'll contact you if the letter you submit will be published. I will also have to contact the writer of the letter, if living, to obtain permission to publish, so I'll need their complete name, address and telephone number as well.

I'm hoping to be overwhelmed with interesting and entertaining letters. What great reading! And I promise to share the best of them all with you. How does this sound for a title? **A Friendly Exchange: America's Personal Letters.**

I'm looking forward to hearing from you.

Lois Barry

c/o Best Letters Press
PO Box 566
La Grande, OR 97850

A Thank You Note

To Susan—best editor, best cheerleader, best friend
This small book needs a larger space for all my gratitude.

Additional thanks to:

Sandy Brown who created my light-filled work space.

Kristin Summers, graphic designer and cheerful collaborator par excellence.

Susan Badger-Jones, Mary McCombs, George Venn and all my other valued correspondents, most of whom will be making cameo appearances in *Delicious Conversations*.

Greg Allen, Kate Allison, Christina Ammon, Mary Brown, Simonne deGlee, Fran Hayden, Carol Larkin, Harry Lonsdale, Tom and Suzanne Madden, Ed Marquand, Lee and Al McGlinsky, Judy Ouderkirk, Sharon Porter, Lynne Sampson, Lyle Schwarz, and my beloved adult children and sharp-eyed husband, all of whom have contributed their interest with many helpful suggestions.

United States Postal Service. Letter writers depend on you.

CPSIA information can be obtained
at www.ICGtesting.com
Printed in the USA
BVOW09s0934171217
503025BV00003B/132/P

9 780982 390405